# MARY:
## A LIFE IN VERSE

by

Patricia Monaghan

DOS MADRES
2014

# DOS MADRES PRESS INC.
P.O.Box 294, Loveland, Ohio 45140
www.dosmadres.com    editor@dosmadres.com

Dos Madres is dedicated to the belief that the small press is essential
to the vitality of contemporary literature as a carrier of the new voice,
as well as the older, sometimes forgotten voices of the past. And in an
ever more virtual world, to the creation of fine books pleasing to the
eye and hand.

Dos Madres is named in honor of Vera Murphy and Libbie Hughes,
the "Dos Madres" whose contributions have made this press possible.

Dos Madres Press, Inc. is an Ohio Not For Profit Corporation and a
501 (c) (3) qualified public charity. Contributions are tax deductible.

Executive Editor: Robert J. Murphy

Illustration & Book Design: Elizabeth H. Murphy
www.illusionstudios.net

Typset in Adobe Garamond Pro, Celtic Garamond the 2nd,
& Hoefler Text
ISBN 978-1-939929-08-2
Library of Congress Control Number:  2014935343

*First Edition*

# ILLUSTRATIONS

For my mother, Mary Monaghan

# INTRODUCTION BY MICHAEL MCDERMOTT

*Mary, a Life in Verse* is a collection written over many years. It was finished but yet without a publisher when my beloved wife Patricia died on November 11, 2012. She had worked finalizing the story over her last years both before and during her illness. She finished poems and the connecting verse narratives during this time. She shared these with me and we began to make plans for publication.

Mary had been an important figure through all periods of Patricia's life. In 1946 Patricia was named Mary Patricia Monaghan as was the custom in many Irish Catholic families for the first born girl. She experienced the emphasis on Mary, like many young Catholic girls, wondering which classmate this May would put the flower crown on the statue of Mary while everyone sang, "Oh Mary, we crown thee with flowers today/ Queen of the Angels, Queen of the May". Here was the hint of a figure more seasonal and universal. Patricia's mother, also Mary, routinely suggested a rosary together when there was a problem or need. The family in Anchorage, Alaska attended Our Lady of Guadalupe church.

Patricia carried Mary involuntarily with her throughout her life and spiritual journey. Impressed and oppressed by woman's place in the Church and society, Patricia, like many during the 60's and 70's, took the paths of feminism and older spiritual traditions. She sought to uncover and bring out the history of women of power and divinity in her poetry and scholarship and create in the present, new practices drawing on this history. Her reaction to the Church was such that she could not enter one, even to attend friends' life events.

Mary's hold and complexity for Patricia was revealed in the 80's. The first edition of her ground breaking and fundamental text, *The Encyclopedia of Goddesses and Heroines,* came out in 1981. In this edition she portrayed Mary as a figure based on ancient Middle Eastern goddesses and then used by the Church to capture the continuing attraction of these beliefs and transform them into a Christian context.

Later in the 80's she came to a friend, embarrassed and unsure, telling her that she had a collection of poems about the Blessed Virgin. As a feminist, Patricia had grown up with and rejected the image of Queen of Heaven and pure virgin as the highest calling for all young women. Yet she told her friend she couldn't get Mary out of her mind and heart. She had, almost against her beliefs of the time, been unable to resist the story that began there and resulted in this book. Her friend and she discussed how, rather than the distant Queen of Heaven and perpetual virgin, a Mary of her time, sharing the life of ordinary women, became the woman of the poems. Her friend, another Irish Catholic, and she agreed that this picture was one they felt was more real and welcome. This would be a Mary closer to how she actually was and less of what was instrumental to the church to hold the faithful and create an image for women in line with its view. The poems were resurrected these few years ago and the collection finished.

Homes, practices and workshops all reflected the continued and increasing presence of Mary. The office and kitchen are to this day adorned with pictures, statues and alters to Mary and a favorite photo print is presented here on page 35. Looking over the land above the valley is a statue in a Mary garden. Returning from Ireland, discussing a new book on goddesses, we found details on the Collrydians who were a group in Thrace in 4th century perhaps lasting into the Middle Ages who upheld and worshipped Mary as divine. After more research, Patricia presented her annual workshop at the priestess gathering of the Reformed Congregation the Goddess. Discussing music for the event, we decided on the Beatles Let It Be, promoting the active involvement of Mother Mary. Small cakes were prepared according to the tradition of the Collrydians. During the workshop many, particularly those raised

Catholic, were in tears over the connections between their deep memories and their present path to the sacred.

The recently published 4th edition of Goddesses and Heroines entry on Mary continues the theme of the relation to goddess figures and stresses that many of the Marion holidays, fall on what were pagan celebrations, including Christmas, Mayday, the Assumption (harvest) and the Presentation (falls on Feb 2, the date of Imbolc). The entry however goes in some detail reviewing the traditional Marion stories and stressing that few of them have a biblical basis. The stories listed there serve as the basis for many of the events portrayed in this collection.

The open acceptance of this syncretized view could be seen when travelling to other cities. If there were a church near our destination we would often enter, go the Mary altar, light candles and pray.

On the day I met Patricia almost exactly 10 years ago, I took her for a drive in the country of the Driftless Area of Wisconsin. I took her to a chapel north of Plain, Wisconsin called Our Lady of Fields. I had been there before. Built by Irish immigrants here shortly after the famine, I was sure Patricia would appreciate and approve of the figure outside holding a sheaf of grain much like Ceres the Roman goddess of agriculture. Inside Mary alone was the dominant figure of the chapel. We knelt and prayed. I had read in *The Red Haired Girl From the Bog*, her spiritual geography of Ireland, that Mary along with Brigit are the main figures close to the people. We began our life together from that journey. It was special place that was the last place we enjoyed going to immediately before her journey here ended.

Mary Patricia Monaghan was proud of this book and the spiritual and artistic journey it represented. Looking deeper, there is much to see beyond dogma in many Marion figures whether the Virgin of Guadalupe and her relation to the Aztec goddess Tonantzin or the Blessed Virgin Mary. This is a book that is respectful of Mary's humanity and the enormity of her task. Some interpretations may be controversial such as Jesus' denial of his mother but all are within the historical tradition. There is some stress on this point particularly because research reminded Patricia that women of the time and culture had absolutely no rights to home or even livelihood when they were widowed. Mary is a figure to be reclaimed and celebrated in her role as mother and as a human woman.

Patricia's work will continue and this is one way. Read and take heart.

Michael McDermott
Brigit Rest, Black Earth Wisconsin
February, 2014

# TABLE OF CONTENTS

## GLORY

ALL THIS HAPPENED LONG AGO. And yesterday. And the day before yesterday. And it will all happen again.

Not this way, exactly. Not exactly this way. But with joy and sorrow and glory. The kind of joy, sorrow and glory you find in any ordinary life. Any ordinary life with its small gifts and immense losses.

Think of that. All those countless lives lived in little towns, in little houses. Lives to which little attention is paid. Lives like mine.

I am old now, and invisible like all old women are. Friend, if you passed me in the market, would you notice? No. You would not. How do I know? Because you were there beside me, yesterday, when I bought a handful of nuts. And the day before, on the street, when I stumbled on a stone. Twice last week, we passed, and you did not meet my eyes.

You don't remember? No matter. I know who I am and what my life means. I know the truth.

Truth? Truths. Some of which contradict others. Just as my presence, the fact that I still live, contradicts the truth of my death long ago.

Where am I? I am right beside you. And nowhere. I am in heaven, if you believe in heaven. Just as I have been in hell, if you believe in hell. Let me tell you all about it. Truthfully. As truthfully as one can tell of mysteries.

# JOY

## ANNUNCIATION

To you it seems a foregone
conclusion, the obvious outcome,
the only possible answer.
Who could say no to an angel?

But there was a moment when I
hesitated.  I remember a wild desire
to be left alone, to be obscure again
and safe—I wanted the angel to leave,

to find some other girl for his strange
invitation.  I was frightened. I heard
a sound like fabric rending or
the tearing of flesh or a great tree

falling.  And yet: I answered.
I leaned towards the angel
and, with a sound like wings,
the future was born in me.


## THE PHENOMENOLOGY OF ANGELS

How could I tell?  He could
have been just a man standing there
while the desert wind lifted
my hair and a snatch of music
drifted in from the street.

How did I know?  I could have
been a woman deceiving myself
that he was more than just a man,
that the blazing day was more than
ordinary, that it changed my life.

Why did I go on?  The day turned
dim.  Think of that: dim.
The sun fading in his radiance.
It was his smile, I think.
That, and the set of his hip.


## TRYING TO MEMORIZE THE ANGEL

For days I sat spinning
on the spot where it had

happened, staring at the place
I had seen the angel incline

towards me, drenching my mind
in the colors of that moment,

tracing the vision over and over.
I wanted never to forget that beauty.

And for a time I remembered, for a time
I could almost touch those soft wings. But

now there's just a picture, a perfect
portrait of an angel holding a pose,

and the spirit has seeped away, all that
angel grace, that luminosity, that fire.

Oh angel, angel!  Even as you stood
there I knew I would forget you!


AND THEN IT WAS OVER, and I was changed, and
the world was changed, and a girl rose from a low bench
beside a window where she had been sitting, looking out
the window onto a desert street when someone inclined his
head towards her and the world shifted—

that girl moved into the cool interior of the room, putting
down her spindle and pulling her robe closer around her
shoulders.  There was nothing in her face or in her body
that looked different from a few moments before, she was
still an ordinary young woman, you would never have
known she had agreed to bring forth the future—

even though I was shattered from the force of it, even
though I felt it on me like a brand, even though I was
changed utterly—there was no roar about me, no halo over
me.

Nothing had changed. Everything had changed.

A breeze brushed my skin.  It felt like wings.


## MARY DESCRIBES THE ANGEL TO ELIZABETH

Imagine the look of a man
who will never be a husband:
he had a special thinness,
a resistance to being fed.
He roused in me such freedom!

And when he moved, it was
with the fresh angularity
of adolescence, even though
he was old, old, his skin
sheer as glass, fragile.

He roused in me such fire!
And oh, yes, I was willing.
I told him, "I will." I did not
mean, "I will do this thing."
I meant, "I will it. I will it."


## MAGNIFICAT

How does a man feel power? Where
does it rest, for him? Does it feel
as it does for us? Is it like this:

There is the power of the head,
when light seems to stream
from thought like hair; and

tongue power, when eloquence strikes;
and the power of hands to mold and
create; and the power of legs to stand

strong and not be moved; and belly's
transformative power; and breasts' power
to give forth; and the ocean power of sex—

And the greatest of all: there are times
when I am whole, when I dance
with each breath and each word,

when my consciousness dwells in all
my parts at once.  When that happens,
I am earth, I am stars, I incarnate god.


## THE PLACE OF WOMAN

Between the ineffable and the unborn
I am.  Between the memory of beauty

and the possibility of its resurrection,
I am.  Between sweetness and sorrow,

between illumination and its object,
I am.  This is my place, this my choice:

not if I will perform a mission,
not if I will take on a task,

but if I can stand here like this, *axis
mundi*, the past swirling into futures

about me, if I can hold power long
enough for a world to emerge from me.


THEY HAVE SURROUNDED ME for years, for ages.
They look like dreams or paintings now, but they were real
in their time, as I was real in mine.  Somehow I remained
while they dissolved, their pain and promise lost.  Those
girls, those girls.

Every woman becomes pregnant through a miracle. Every
one of those girls like me—alone, abandoned, poor, hope-

less, homeless—every one carries the secret of the future.
Even those who refuse the angel—even they are holy.

I was alone and poor, silent with mystery, my body ripen-
ing like a pomegranate.

So many like me, so many millions of girls, fresh as dew,
beautiful as doves.  Some were refused food and died, some
were pelted with stones and died, some were thrown in the
sea and died.

Some lived, but their children were taken from them.
Some lived, but their children were killed.  Some lived,
happy in the sound of their children's voices, but selling
their bodies for bread.

Only a few found shelter.  I was one of the lucky ones.

When my son said, "what you do to the least of them,"
whom did you imagine that he meant?


## THE BEGINNING OF STORY

It is not that I cannot say what happened.
It is not that words diminish it.
It is not that I would be misunderstood.

At the furthest reaches of beauty the senses
lose their memory. The eye cannot hold
the light. The music slides away.

When I try to say what I saw
words do not fail: memory fails,
vision fails, the senses fail.

When I try to say what I know, I say
things completely other.  Now a story
exists, and it is not what occurred.

What I saw was not beautiful. It was beauty.
What I heard was not true.  It was truth.
What I am saying now is less that what I know.


NOT EVEN DUTIFUL JOSEPH believed me.  He
was a proud man, and kind, and conventional as old men
often are. We had been betrothed before the angel came.
He would not go back on his word.

I do not blame him, not now, not from this distance, for
his anger.  He was a man of his world, of his time.  He
could not be otherwise, just as I was a woman of my time
and could not be otherwise.

I told him one day in the cool inner garden, knowing
that he had the right to turn me away.   And he imagined
what any man would: that I had lain with a man, not him,
and conceived a child, not his.  He could not imagine the
unimaginable.

And perhaps he was right.  Perhaps, after all, I had cre-
ated an impossible story to hide what some would call my
shame.  But I do not feel shame now.  I felt none then.

What did I feel?  Baffled, I think, amazed.  I could not
explain the mystery of how I came to stand before Joseph,
my belly softening before hardening with child, just as I
cannot explain why he acted as he did.

He felt betrayed but would not betray me. He told me
that, turning quickly so that I would not see his mouth
twist as though he were eating bitter fruit.

Soon my nipples grew dark. My belly grew hard.  Old
women teased us both.  Joseph's eyes grew hard and dark.
But he kept his word, and my secret.


## THE BEAUTY OF THE WORLD

For a time, as though the angel shadowed
the world with light, everything was radiant.
The faces, the bodies, of men, of women,

were illuminated.  I was in love with
the world.  I felt included in all lives.
I saw unearthly light shining through

all things.  Then one day, it all grew dim.
No one passed me in the market smiling
that bright smile, no faces were lit

with meaning, beauty hid itself
in mortality and time.  I darkened too
and stopped trying to see angels.


## NATIVITY SCENE

Afterwards I heard people say how easy
it had been for me, how painless,

how Eve's curse had been lifted for me,
just this once, how much more

difficult it always had been for others—
another's fortune opens opportunity

for such complaint—and everyone said
how beautiful, how beautiful.  And that

was true.  And it was true, too, about
the pain.  There was so little, if

tearing precognition of loss
does not count as pain, and if

a crushing sense of love and doom
does not count as suffering.

Yes, it was easy for me.  Painless.
Exactly as you imagined.


ACCORDING TO THE LAW, I was impure.  Had
been impure for 40 days.  And why?  Because I'd given
birth.  Which marked me as unclean, tainted, polluted and
defiled.

I never felt that way, not for a moment in the time it took
the moon to move from new to full and back to new
again, then back once more towards full.  Yet I was called
impure.

We waited in Bethlehem. Joseph found some distant cousins there. It was too far to Nazareth to make that journey until after the ceremony. We made camp in an olive grove near my husband's family. Everyone loved the baby. It was a happy time.

The morning after the second full moon, I went to the temple. I went the way women have followed rituals they did not believe for millennia. The way they follow them today. Because it is expected. Because we're told to. Because there seems no way out.

It was a sin against myself, my knowing heart. Is it any wonder that, right at the door, I met a man who foretold death and pain?


## DEPARTURE

I had just begun to accept
the humanness of it all—

that lost radiance had become
a vague dream, not even memory—

when you returned. I was walking
back from the market, and the day

was bright and hot, and people were
chatting, and music played distantly

and you appeared. I stared at you.
You stared back. I turned my head

away and told myself no, this
cannot be, this is not angel, this is

just a man. Then I turned back and
looked again.  It was you.  Here—

oh, just when life was bearable
again—you, again, here.  A warning?

A reminder?  I ran.  When I looked back
over my shoulder, you were watching.

That night, I realized why you'd come.
We heard the rumors and escaped.


IN EGYPT, HEARING OF THE SLAUGHTER

Last night we saw a traveler.
Even at a distance, we knew
he was from home: his clothing,
the songs he sang as he walked.

Last night the traveler stayed
at our fire, ate our meal with us,
refreshed us with the laughter
of our tongue, then told us the news.

For the first time I left my child
and walked out to the desert night.
I walked for hours, bruising my feet
on the hidden stones.  I lay on a hill

beneath a dead tree.  The sand was
still warm from the day.  I saw light
puncture the sky like knife-tears in flesh.
For the first time, I hated the angel.


I COULD HAVE BEEN ONE who suffers little joy,
little pain, one who redeems nothing, is guilty of nothing.
Except for that instant when I felt power spread through
my body.

It was in my flesh, not in my soul, that the miracle took
place. Life shone through my body. At the moment I
agreed, I embodied love and power.  Rivers rose in flood
with my tears, the sea grew hot with my lust, the wind bat-
tered in fury when I raged.

I became the world. I had no doubts that this child was
intended by every power I knew.

Oh, angels toy with us so!

From here—from this heaven, this dream, wherever this
is—I can see what I did not see then. In the ages that have
passed since I was a mother, I have learned such bitter
truths. That for every child beloved and desired, a dozen
are not. That my experience was not that of every mother,
every child.

From this heaven, from this dream, I see infants exposed
or strangled or suffocated. Mostly girls. No one counts
them, no one has counted them in all the years since I left
the earth. All those innocents, outnumbering the desert
sands.

17

The boys do not escape, even if they live. Herod killed them in their swaddling clothes. But mostly kings let them grow up, then kill them in wars and persecutions, and they keep on killing them and killing them. The slaughter of innocents goes on, and on, and on.


## SAFE, IN AN UNFAMILIAR LAND

In the market, small green
fruits and yellow berries and
slabs of a coarse bread.

I do not know their names.
I say, "that," and point.
A woman of another tribe

wearing a robe embroidered
in unfamiliar colors smiles and
fills my hand. I cannot thank her.

I am safe here, among words
that hold no memories. Here
there is no blood, no weeping.


## IN THE DESERT

Here the people say,
I am thirsty for love,
and, I thirst to see you.
They speak of raging thirst,
ravening thirst, gnawing thirst.

It is different at home, where
there is always enough water
but never enough food. There,
we say "I hunger for truth" or
"I hunger for love."

Here, I am learning
to say, "I thirst for release,"
to say, "I thirst for my mother,"
to say, "I thirst for home."
Yes, I thirst for home.


OUR LOVE BEGAN IN THE DESERT. In the cold
nights, Joseph opened his cloak to me. I drew comfort and
warmth from him, and he, from me. Far from home, with
only each other and the child, we nested in each other.

When you have loved an angel, what is an old man? How
could I compare a lined face and a hunched back to the
radiance of heaven?

How could I find him beautiful? An old man who wore
his skin like an ill-fitting shroud? An old man whose eyes
were dim and cloudy, whose hair was thin and white?

And yet.

One night, under uncountable stars and a bright moon,
the babe awakened me. I sat up to offer him my breast and
there, as the night breeze stroked my skin, I looked down
on Joseph's heaving chest. He coughed slightly in his sleep,
and my heart swelled. His goodness made me soften, and
his sturdy care for us.

At that moment, I became his wife. The rest came later.

## HOME TO NAZARETH

Look: here it is,
my mother's comb.
And here is the small
brass mirror with
its reed handle

and here, the tablecloth
I was weaving that day
with its bright blue threads
captured by bands of red—

I must bring water
from the village well
to wash these gray green
dishes and this dusty floor.


WE RETURNED, THE CHILD, THE MAN
AND I, and life began to dream through us its consoling
rhythms, each day opening its monotonous expectedness
to us, a bazaar of little likelihoods—

the child's dawn cry, Joseph's first stirrings as he rose in the
dim clattering morning, then my daily work: grinding the
meal, baking the flat loaves, drawing cold water in noon
heat, rush-scouring the wood floor,

Joseph pounding in the courtyard on a cart or a cot or a
table, the boy eyeing a spider that swung from the window,
punching a finger at it,

and I made soup and Joseph a shelf, and the child discov-
ered the delights of screaming, and I ground the meal and
baked the loaves, drew water and scoured the floor,

and the peace of the ordinary fell on us like a coverlet that
warms and hides and protects, the peace of ordinary life
defying death moment by moment by moment.

## MIRACLES

The most extraordinary
things happen:

we have enough to eat.
We have a home.
We hold each other in
the warm nights.
The baby is healthy
and smiles like stars.
We are all alive.

We have fresh eggs,
hardy parsley,
milk, and flowers.

I sit spinning and
watch him play.
He watches clouds
through the window,
pointing to the sky.
He giggles and gurgles.
I put my spindle
down, caught by his
miraculous smile.

## LIFE AFTER ANGELS

In stories, angels are important,
and massacres, and near escapes.

But life is not a story.  Life is one
unremarkable day after another:

it is spring, I have filled
the house with flowers, breezes

cool our bodies every night
and our son smiles and smiles.

## THE SILENT YEARS

It was not God I birthed.
It was a child, a joyous
infant, fragile and smiling
who grew into a boy

so strong, so agile.
He brought me such joy
that I pretended that
I had not seen our future.

In memory now those
days are shadowed by loss.
But then, I loved him
with no cloud and no cross,

just the passionate bond
of body to body.  When he sucked
at my breast, when he clung
to my hand, I felt nothing but

the dance of the spirit,
the leap of the soul. I thought
we could outwit death.
I believed he'd grow old.


I LOST HIM IN JERUSALEM, TWICE. Each time,
three days.  But that first time, he returned to me.

We had gone to Jerusalem for Passover and were beginning
the long walk north to Nazareth. We could not find our
son, so we assumed he was already on he road.  But when
we reached home, he was not there.

We did what any parents would: turned back, returned
to where we left him.  It took days to return, but we were
confident and unconcerned.  But he was not there.

The next day, we retraced our steps around the city. Passover was done, the visitors gone home, Jerusalem quiet. Surely he had gone here? Gone there? The city was small. We began to imagine accident, loss, death, and we said no, no, no, he is nearby, we are looking in the wrong place.

The third day, we walked the dusty streets again. Joseph's head was bowed. This was his son, child of his heart, who was missing. I walked beside him slowly, repeating "not now, not now," and seeing the face of Simeon the Prophet.

Simeon was dead, but my memory of his prophecy drew me to the temple. And there stood our boy, preaching and debating. He was enjoying himself. While we sought and suffered! My anger and my love were equal at that moment.

As we walked the long road back to Nazareth, our son boasting of how he bested the Temple scholars, I thought of only two things: that someday, he would leave for good, and that somewhere, another woman was searching for a child she would never find.


THE PROPHECY RECALLED

I remembered at the strangest times:
when I smoothed his tangled hair
or when he ran in panting from play,
when he slept and I memorized
every shadow on his face,

never when he wanted something,
or when he fixed me with those
pleading eyes, not when he was
ashamed of himself and hid,
not when we laughed together

but in the odd oblique moments
when his attention was
elsewhere and mine on him,
I remembered what the old man
said: that I would see him die.

# SORROW

THERE IS LIFE BEFORE SORROW, and life afterwards.

He was older than me.  I always expected to live beyond him.
But even knowing, I was not prepared.  How can one prepare
for the unknowable?

I tried.  When we planted olive trees beside our home, I imag-
ined them grown, him gone, me alone.  When I wove him a
new cloak, I imagined sewing him into his shroud.  When he
held me in the cool still night, I imagined his dying breaths,
first shallow and slow, then ceasing.

He was an old man, Joseph, when we wed.  He told me I made
him young, but I did not.  He grew older, older.

And then he died, there among his tools and lumber.  It was
nothing like I imagined.  I heard a crashing sound.  I found
him slumped across the table, just moments gone.  I did not
hear his final breath or see what words his mouth formed at the
end.  I cradled his gray head as it grew cold.

I cried, but only later.  First I made a shroud of his best cloak.
As evening came, we buried him under those tall olive trees.

This was how it began, my season of sorrow.


## THE LIMITS OF STORY

Our story: now I know the way it ends.
No longer can I dream the path will bend
and lead us round and home again.

No longer can I think that we will walk
this autumn by the salt-dead sea and talk
of little matters.  We will never hear the cock

greet dawn again, nor watch the night begin,
nor break bread together, nor share a skin
of new sweet wine.  Never again.

It is over. The door is closed, the scroll
complete.  And me?  Shall I grow old
without him?  A story yet to be told.


## RESURRECTION

Someone cut down our
almond tree. It is spring.
The tree was in full bud.

It stood in an open field, in no
one's way.  Needless death.
I could not stop weeping.

A week later the buds
opened into sprays of white
and for a moment I thought

that bees would come and
fertilize these flowers
and there might yet be fruit

this year—what folly, to
imagine immortality—flowers
are resurrection enough.

AND NOW, MORE SORROW. My son. Gone. To the desert. To pray, he says. For what? He could not say.

For eighteen years, I had forgotten prophecies and angels. I loved my husband and our son's bright smile. We lived simply, day to day, day by day. From here, from now, I see how close to heaven such a simple life can be, when there is bread enough, and love, and good work to fill the days.

Then Joseph died. An earthquake, shattering my foundations. Then the aftershock. I thought our son would pick up his father's tools, that we would live together in his father's house. I was not ready to be alone. I was not ready to be homeless.

But my son went about his father's business.

That night, the lepers came. They stood beside the door, hands out. I gave them bread and lentils. Then I saw the child's sore bleeding foot and the mother's raw red arms, and I went back inside and picked up all Joseph's clothes— all of them, he had no further need of them—and brought them outside.

Here, I said, take his good cloak and his favorite shoes, and his soft linen loincloths—yes, even those most intimate of rags—and wear them until they are threadbare and torn, filthy and dark, then burn them,

burn them far away from me and my once-happy home.


THERE IS SO MUCH YOU DO NOT KNOW about me, you who call me "mother." You who call me "virgin." You who call me "queen."

31

From here, I watch you invent lives for me, ones that suit your needs. But when I call out to you like a leper, you close the door.

You look up to heaven, but I live beside you, starving, hurt, abandoned. I stare out from the eyes of the girl doomed to be sold into an old man's bed. I am the homeless mother, hiding from the knife. The old one, raving in mindless pain, shunted aside, ignored.

You light candles and sing hymns to someone with my name, someone I never was. And I wipe the tears of the world, I who shed so many, so many, so many.

When my son left, I was cast out. Under law, I could not inherit. I used the little coin I had to buy widow's clothes, as the law required. Then I had nothing.

I could beg. Most widows did. Or I could find someone to take me in, to bake bread, haul water, sweep the hard dirt floor. My parents were long dead. Joseph's family lived in Bethlehem. There was nowhere else to turn.

I took a little bread and set out under a darkening sky.

Poor women walk. I see them all the time, walking in rain and snow and scorching heat, through forests, over deserts. I see them now, on broken pavements and dusty trails, I see them sore and aching, walking. Poor women walk, they always have.

And so I walked. Down the plain of Esdraelon beneath Mount Tabor. I walked in fear through the valley of Jezreel, land of the Samaritans. To the River Jordan, to

Jericho, to the valley of the shadow of death. I walked for
weeks, a poor woman struggling along a dusty road. To
Bethlehem, again.


## CAMPED BY THE OASIS

In a moment of presence
when the past was open to me
and the future came like space
toward me, I listened to the palms

as they gossiped among themselves
of the Armageddon of the sun
they had just passed through,
of how thirst made their roots weaken,

and of the deep drink possible
in certain seasons, and of the round
of merry song the spring wind brings,
and of the sweet sleep of winter—

and how twenty rounds ago they swelled
all together in a perfect year, and how
forty years ago they built thin rings
around themselves in fearsome drought.

I heard all this one evening beneath the trees,
and felt my heart open after grief,
open to vast minds and thick bodies,
open to the slowly bluing sky.

## BETHLEHEM, AGAIN

I have come all this distance,
walking under the fierce sky
in the grip of a dim vision.
What did I expect to find?

In all those years, I had not
remembered a tree, tilting sharply
near a rock, until I saw it again. How
much I had forgotten.  How it all

comes back: the way the dialect is
different here. That faint spice
fragrance we do not have at home.
The way memory is sight and sound,

scent and taste, the way that
that memory lives in the body.
In Bethlehem, I am still a girl.
In Bethlehem, there are still angels.


WHY DID I NOT GO WITH HIM?  SIMPLE: he
never asked.

But I did not mind.  I was about a woman's business, the
actions that sustain the world.  Without such work, who
would eat, who would drink cool water drawn from a vil-
lage well, who would hold fast a cloak against the wind?

Only those who have never taken a sheared skin, carded
it, spun it, then wove it into heavy cloth, would think my
work unimportant.  Only those who do not know what

water weighs, or how long it takes to winnow wheat, could
think my life was easy.

I see how things have changed.  If I lived today, in some
lands I could be an artist or a merchant or a priest.  I might
like that.  I might be good at that.  But I might live the
way I lived before, living as most women do, caring and
tending.

And there is good in that.  Though I made no laws and
wrote no poems, my life had meaning, value, worth.  And
not because I bore a child—not even that one, whom you
worship.  My life was good because I lived it, and I loved.


## A NEW PLACE IN THE OLD

It was winter, dry and chill.
From the north across the sea
came the winter winds.
I sat beneath a lime tree
spinning.  Winter is a good

time for that, especially the cool
nights after the market grows
silent, when the doves coo
in the rafters.  Years passed
like that, in the consolation

and profundity of routine.
Joseph's family was kind.
I was useful.  Life was good.
I heard from my son now
and then.  I dreamed.  I lived.

IN THOSE PUBLIC YEARS I heard, now and again, where he was, who traveled with him, what he preached. I heard how Elizabeth's son John baptized him, declaring him the savior. Poor John, dead so soon at Herod's hand, his head displayed like a trophy. And yet, like me, like my son, the Baptist lives on. I saw him on the street today, muttering as he always did, brilliant and deranged and prophetic all at once. I saw the way you passed with averted eyes, not even giving a coin to the holy man.

If the savior were to come again, would you embrace him? Would those in power welcome him?

I heard my son had settled with his friends, not far from Nazareth, at Capernaum on the Sea of Galilee. I sent word that I now lived in Bethlehem. I wondered if he worried about me. I worried about him, as any mother would.

Then an old friend's daughter married. It was a long walk, back to Nazareth and on to Cana. To my surprise, my son was there. It had been several years since I had seen him. He seemed much older. He sat with me. He told me of his friends, his prayers, his visions. And then I noticed guests calling for more wine, and servants hiding behind curtains so they did not have to answer. My poor relations had nothing more to give.

I told my son. He shrugged. I told the servants to do what he said. He shrugged again. But like a good son, he gave directions. Six stone jugs of water. Then six stone jugs of wine.

I had known angels. Of course I expected miracles.

## HE DENIES ME THREE TIMES

Once, I tried to see him when
he was preaching.  Someone

called out to him that I was there.
"Who is my mother?" he asked.

"Whoever does the will of God
is my brother and sister and mother."

Another time, he passed through
Nazareth, and someone asked,

"Are you not Mary's son?"
And he responded, "Prophets

are without honor in their own
country and in their own house."

And then the final one.  A crowd
listening to him.  Someone calls out,

"Blessed is the womb that bore you
and the breasts that nursed you!"

And he responds, "Blessed rather are those
who hear the word of God and obey."

He was about his father's business.
I understood.  And yes, I wept.

I WEPT AND WENT ON WITH MY LIFE. Years passed. I was content with my lot, cleaning and spinning for others. I heard enough of my son to know he was safe. More and more, people talked of him. They told me his message of humility and love. I was proud of him. I missed him, but I was proud.

The next part of the story, you think you know already. You hold a picture in your mind of me beneath a cross, looking up in pure sweet pain. But do you know the rest?

He came to Jerusalem, just a few miles away from me. Even in Bethlehem, we heard how he rode into the city on a donkey, not on a warrior's horse, a simple gesture of peace. My son! I was eager to see him, this man who preached against greed, who told us we should be leaven to help others rise, who called himself the good shepherd. I packed my things and walked to the holy city.

It was Passover. Jerusalem was crowded. Everyone knew of my son's arrival, but no one knew where he was. I walked through the markets, a poor widow asking for help. Most people ignored me. Those who answered me, knew nothing. I never knew where he ate his Seder supper. I did not drink the wine, I did not eat unleavened bread, I did not hear the words "do this in remembrance of me." I slept outdoors, huddled in my cloak, and sought my son in the crowded streets.

Then I heard a merchant tell the news of how the governor had ruled. I ran through the streets to Golgatha.

AND NOW WE REACH THE CENTER. I stand,
barely moving, beneath a cross where a man is slowly dying.
You have seen this picture so many times: the gloomy sky,
the other dying men, the spear headed for my son's heart.

The most important moment. As you tell the story.

For me, three hours of eternity. Death hovering like the
stormy clouds, like the milling crowd. A passion that moves
towards an inevitable ending, whose time you cannot know.

The moment of salvation, as you tell the story.

My story is different. Yes, this scene is central, for before it,
I was a mother.

A man whose mother dies is an orphan. What is the word
for a woman whose only child has died?

And that was not the only change. Before Golgatha, I
believed. An angel unfolded my life to me, and I believed.
But on that skull hill, belief died with my son. What was
my life, once he had died?


## THE THIRD HOUR

There were
moments—yes
I confess it—

when I willed
him to live—
even pierced

41

with nails,
even crowned with
thorns—to inhale

one more
pain-wracked breath—
anything but death—

anything but
a world without
him, eyes shut

forever, the light
gone, forever—
never

to hear him
speak again—
his limbs

were twisted
in pain, and
I insisted

on one more
breath, one more,
one more—


## AND THEN, IT WAS OVER.

You may have heard that my son spent the next three days
in hell.  That he descended to the underworld and freed
the souls held there.

I cannot say if that is true.  I was not there.  I was on earth: alive, alone, bereaved.

The instant he died, I felt swaddled in peace.  I was calm and tearless.  The instant he died, I felt holy, wholly enveloped by love.

An hour later I was in hell.

I had held him when he was born, amazed at the stranger who peered back at me, curious and loving.  I held him when he died, amazed at the absence in his staring eyes.

What is hell?  To be a mother and to hold your only child, his head falling back, his mouth open in a small frozen circle, his eyes still open.

I could not cry, not yet.  I just held him as his body stiffened and grew cold.

Perhaps he went to hell.  I know I did.


THE HARROWING OF HELL

Everything burned.
Even water.  My heart
was a ball of red flame.

I was seared and raw.
I was covered with boils.
I was blistered with grief.

My blood was venom.
My tears were poison.
My breath was a scourging wind.

Blind with pain,
I fell against sharp
thorns and bled.

Around me, I heard
soft cries.  Around me
I heard muffled moans.

*

Then there was a plain
gray and flat,
treeless, featureless,
endless.

Then there was a plain
where I walked and walked
and walked and walked
and passed nothing.

Then there was a plain
dry and tearless.
Then there was a plain
dull and endless.

Then there was a plain.

*

And from a dead white pit
a rail of ice flew up, I stepped
on it and was impaled,

twitching and gasping, blood
pooling under me, unable
to lift myself high enough
to pull free, unable to
break the ice needled inside
my legs—I fell past it,
wrapped in myself and my pain,
and felt it absorbed into my
spine, my ice spine, and disappear.

*

Between molten lakes
of red lava are deserts
of blistering sand and
fiery wind and
a cold vacant sky,
where nothing moves
nothing breathes,
no heart beats,
and I do not want
to try to move past
the desert stretches
because I know
that swimming in molten
rock is my only choice.

Dimly, around me, I see others:
a man with his feet on fire,
a man whose stomach grows
through a whole in his hide,
a child whose flesh is torn
endlessly by angry red ants,
a woman with no bones.
When they see me, what

do they see? A woman
with a hole in her chest
and no arms, a woman
with no eyes, only running sores,
a woman whose hair blazes
from her head in a corona of pain.

## LOSING FAITH

All my life, I held the angel's secret.

I believed, I believed.

All the angel said, I believed.

I never doubted.

Then I stopped believing.

Sudden as night, and as dark.


## OTHERS SAY THEY HAVE SEEN HIM

The others say they have seen him.
The others say they have felt
his presence like a wind in the room.
The others say he lives still, or lives again.

But I have not seen him.   I have not
heard his dear voice. I have not
felt him like a ball of fire, like
a sighing wind, like a bright shadow.

Why has he not come? Why them,
not me?  Does he not want to comfort me?
If he lives, anywhere in any form
in this entire universe, would he not

come and wrap his arms around me
and quiet my sobs and tell me to believe
in life, would he not wipe my streaming eyes
with his robe and tell me to believe in love,

would he not find me, in this endless
empty universe, find me alone here
and tell me himself that there is
comfort after death, not just peace

but freedom and joy and profound
solitary delight?  How can I believe
what others say, what others saw?
Either he is gone, or has forsaken me.


## WHAT WOULD BE A SIGN?

Thomas doubted, and was offered
a bleeding wound, a hand
dipped into warm living blood,
and doubted no more.

If I doubt strongly enough,
will he come to me too?

## THE RICH WOMAN DESPISES MY TEARS

I went to the temple
like a trusting child
a child who has fallen
and is badly hurt,
who cries as much
with need for comfort
as with pain—

My shoulders shook,
I lifted my sleeve
to wipe my eyes,
and saw her,
the rich woman,
—her Tyrian robe,
her kohl eyes
gesture at me
and laugh.

Her companion glanced
my way, shook her head,
and laughed. My arm,
before my face, froze.

What would he
say to that woman,
to her companion? What
would he say to me?

He would say,
forgive, forgive,
they too are in pain.
They are small
and helpless. He

would say, forgive.
I say, may your
children die and you
stand here weeping,
and may I come in,
brushing past you
in my blue robe,
and toss only
a bent penny
to your grief.


## SHE VISITS JUDAS

He wept when I entered.
He stood before me,
eyes storming, eyes
flooded and dark, and

began to talk wildly
of his reasons, how
it seemed like fate,
how he had always been
weak, how he didn't really

remember what he had done.

I sat next to him, silent,
sun dappling the tree
beside me, wind moving
my robe slightly,
so slightly—

When I left I walked
for hours, raw as
a desert wind, cold
as a bedrock spring.
I was empty, empty.

And then I saw a man
in the market
strike a woman,
and all the pain
in the world
struck me like a blow.

# GLORY

## LIVING THE STORY

If this were a story, this would be
the point when time slows down—

a dark river emptying itself
into a lake as the desert blooms—

this would be the moment when
listeners would know themselves poised

at the edge of ending, and that
the end is happy.  They know this

by the changing glow of sunlight,
by the boat drifting on the lake,

by the softness of the air,
by the suddenness of flowers.

If this were a story, I would release
my breath in a long slow sigh.

But I am living this story,
not telling it, not hearing it,

and in the midst of it I ask:
Will this desert ever bloom?


## TEARS LIKE FLOWERS

They came today, again, as though
some season had called them back,

the tears—freshets of loss that
I once thought would end and be

gone for good—thinking grief a season
that would pass, not knowing the way

it runs through all our days like
an underground river that

rises now and again through rocks
and soft grass, like flowers that

suddenly bud and bloom, following
their own internal clock.  What

brought them now, not yesterday?
Once I looked for causes: that flower,

the color of his robe; that scent,
the myrrh of his birth; the shape

of a cross against a distant sky.
Now I know these are not causes,

only accidents of time, for tears
bloom in their own season,

and now I greet this downpour
like I greet any spring, with joy,

for as long as these tears bloom
upon my cheeks, he is still here.

## A TURNING

Another ordinary day
redolent with sunshine
and the late summer smell
of drying beans and
ripening fruit.

I took the long way
home from the well,
for no special reason.
I passed the home
of a woman I knew.

I stopped and called
through the open door.
No answer. I set down
my heavy water jar
and went inside.

In the courtyard
she sat like a rock,
like a mountain, like
a graven marble image.
She did not speak.

I knew what had
happened. I knew
death had visited
her home. I sat down
and took her hand.

I sat in silence,
holding her cool hand,
as the bright day

turned gray and stormy.
I held my robe

over her head as it
began to rain, as she
began to cry.  I held
her, in the rain, as
night fell on Bethlehem.

Have I now some certain
instinct for death that
I took that road today?
Outside her door, my
water jar spilled over.


I TOOK THE SAME PATH EVERY DAY, walking
at dawn outside the village.  I walked to a flat rock beneath
an ancient olive near a dry stream, sat for a moment to
breathe in the weather and the season, then walked back to
begin my work.

My only solitary time, my cherished hour.

A few days after a storm, when the air was fresh and damp,
I set my feet on the familiar path.  Within moments, every-
thing seemed changed.  Where was my rock, my breathing
space?  What was that sound, like wind in trees?

In the timeless space where I now live, a space of memory
and shadowed light, I ponder the ordinary and the miracu-
lous.  How they are different.  How they are the same. And
I think of that day I got  lost on a familiar path, a day of
ordinary wonders.

The sky reddened, and whispers drew me on. Everything seemed new and sacred. Pebbles gleamed like jewels beneath my feet. The air was full of wings.

Then, just beyond a slight rise, a flood. Water gurgling over stone. The dry stream suddenly running at full spate. There was my tree, my resting place. Nothing was different. Everything was changed.

## MIDNIGHT, SPINNING

It is midnight; even the mice
are asleep. I sit spinning,
the shank of coarse yarn growing

around my spindle, the full

melody of the twisting cords
singing in my mind. Clouds
from the future, and the past,

scud across my mind.
At midnight I sit spinning
the house finally quiet,

I have its silence to myself.

Watching my spindle move,
I float away from the present
to the day all this began.

That afternoon with an angel.

I have had moments of joy
since then, and moments of
the most abject sorrow.

And ordinary sacred hours.


MY LIFE WENT ON.  After the joy, the passion and
the sorrow, life went on.  I went on.

Your stories ignore me after his death and resurrection.
You see me at the cross, that final day, but after that, I grow
faint and ghostly.  But what was the difference from before?
Had I not been invisible for years, living quietly in Beth-
lehem, tending to women's chores, one of the countless
ordinary women of this world?

Once, when I was young, an angel spoke to me. Then,
nothing, year after year after year.  I held a secret in my
heart and built a life around it.  I believed, until my son's
death, that my life was blessed.

And it was blessed, in the way ordinary lives are blessed
with ordinary miracles: the way bread rises and grows
fragrant, the sweet promises of spring, the helpful hand of
a friend.

I had said, let it be.  And afterwards, it was.

And then I saw him die, and I lost faith.  Making mean-
ing out of nothingness was harder, this second time, for
there were no angel messengers, no heavenly radiance, only
death and loss.

I never saw him risen.  Could I believe he walked out of the tomb and ascended to heaven?

At first, I lived in the dimness of doubt.  But then I decided to believe what my heart so yearned to be truth.  Once again, I heard myself say, let it be. And what I believed, became true.

There is glory in renewal.  Wind tears at the trees and at my roof and at my veils.  But when I close my eyes, I see angels.


## THE SAGE FROM THE EAST

He was sitting at the well
at dawn, his eyes raw
with prayer, his body
taut with discipline.

He took a bowl from
beneath his yellow robe
and held it out to me.
I had nothing, I had

only the water I had
just drawn, so I
poured some into his
waiting bowl. He drank,

deep and simple, pure
in his thirst. He did not
thank me. He did not bow.
He did not touch my hand.

He looked past me into
some wavering distance
and told me pain was a veil
between self and spirit,

that beauty trapped me
in further pain, that
I should seek rest in
nothingness, in the abyss.

Some part of me drank,
not purely but in desperate
thirst, some part of me
embraced oblivion's repose.
And yet I did not fill
my bowl from his well.
Knowledge, fine as light,
poured into my soul.

You have forgotten love,
I said to him.  Even spirit—
especially spirit—yearns
towards love, I told him.

I touched his hand.
And radiance flashed
like lightning from him.
For a moment, I saw

beyond the tattered flesh,
beyond the rigid soul,
and into a blue abyss,
a nothingness of self

but filled with love,
filled with him and me,
endlessly full,
endlessly filled.


## HE IS, I AM

Once again autumn ends, the winds
die down on the desert, small mammals
burrow home, gentleness blankets us.

He is still dead, and I am still alive.

Winter draws us inside, to friends
and fires, root vegetables and grain,
stories and old songs and secrets.

I am still alive, and he is still dead.

Spring will come crackling, all buds
and migrations, soon enough, but now
we nestle, nest, knowing, nurturing.

I am still alive.  I am still alive.


## WHAT IS LIFE WITHOUT ANGELS?

Mine came when I was young.  I was so strong, so confi-
dent.  More than I am now.  When the angel spoke, I did
not doubt that I was chosen.  It was only a matter of saying
yes.

That was many years ago. My hair is gray and thin. My belly is round, my arms thin. My eyes nest in wrinkles. I have joined the invisible old. You do not see me, even when I touch your arm. What is my purpose now? Did I complete it with one act, one affirmation, one birth?

Many remembered my son. His followers traveled across the seas, bringing his words with them. But around me, nothing changed. What good was all the labor, all the pain? I believed that he had risen and had conquered death. Could I believe his message of life?

From here, from now, I see how grace spread through the world. The good news spread. The peace of the divine shared among all people, rich and poor, men and women. But not grace alone. Cruelty and ignorance, greed and perversion, all in my son's name. So many hurt, so many dead, at the hands of crusaders and priests. Was it worth it?

I accepted an angel's invitation and loved and suffered afterwards. And ended my life alone. Was it worth it?

What if I had said no? Was there another girl, sleepily waiting for angels to approach? Did I take what might have been hers? Or does every girl have an angel of her own?

But I said yes. And everything unfolded from that word. One ordinary woman, a moment of belief, and the world was changed.

## WATCHING

A butterfly flew past me
in the garden today.

It looked at me.

It looked at me and I felt
the eyes of the universe

watching me.  I looked around
and the lime tree was

watching me.  There were
eyes in the clouds.  Everywhere

I felt a watching presence.
An ant crawled on my foot

and I did not move to
brush him off.


## ALLELUIA

Sitting in the sun outside my house
one day, another gift came to me:
a man walked by, playing a flute.

It was late summer, and leaves
had fallen from the palm
beside the house, and one leaf

leapt up as he passed, leapt up
just as the melody piped sharply
higher, and held that high note,

and the sun winked at that moment,
from behind a cloud, and a sharp
scent of new figs filled the air,

and I was song, suddenly song,
I remembered in my deepest soul
something I had always known:

that our only purpose is to live,
to be the eyes of god watching
this world, seeing all its beauty,

to be god's ears and hear its music,
to be all god's senses, all at once—
to be god's body, and to dance.


I GREW OLD, MY EYES FAILED, my heart grew
weak, I died.

My single blessing was: I lived in memory, talking to the
dead. For in memory my son still lived, and Joseph too,
and Elizabeth and Anna and Joachim, old Simeon the
prophet and wild beheaded John. I was never lonely in
those days. I held converse with my beloved ones, and
they showered me with wisdom and with hope.

Hope? You wonder what hope an obscure aged woman
can have, whose life has been hard work and pain? What
hope except release in death?

Yet my heart sang.  I knew the world.  I could not ignore the sound of a Roman whip on a slave's back, outside my door.  I knew the poor, for I had been poor; I knew the pain of women, for I was one; I suffered for the criminal and outcast, like my son.

There was no reason for song, no reason for hope.  But if we wait for reasons, we will be forever silent, forever hopeless.

I once said yes to an angel.  So I said yes to hope, yes with all of my weakly beating heart.  And with my yes, the world changed.

Or was it me who changed? I passed into the embrace of those I loved, and love grew and grew until I embraced all life.  As I do now, looking at you there, your heart as full of pain and loss as mine once was.

From this heaven, from this dream, from wherever I am now, I embrace you now and tell you: Sing.  Dance.  Hope.  Dream.  Love.
It might change the world, it might not.  But the world will not change unless you do.

## WHAT THEY CALL ME

Ark of the Covenant, Cause of Our Joy,
Dispenser of Grace, Eastern Gate,

Flower of Carmel, Health of the Sick,
House of Gold, Immaculate Mother,

Lady of Sorrows, Mirror of Justice,
Morning Star, Mystical Rose

Queen of Peace, Refuge of Sinners,
Rose Ever Blooming, Seat of Wisdom,

Star of the Sea, Tower of Ivory,
Woman Clothed With the Sun.

I am all of that and more.
I am none of that and less.

I am as you are: a woman who
lived and loved and suffered.


## BEATITUDES

Blessed is the air that breathes us, that we breathe.
Blessed is water that fills and drowns and quenches.

Blessed is earth that sustains and upholds.
Blessed are mountains, beautiful and treacherous.

Blessed are oceans, roads and barriers.
Blessed are islands, distant and contained.

Blessed are trees that shade and feed.
Blessed are fruits, nuts, stalks and roots.

Blessed are birds and beasts and snakes.
Blessed: butterflies, spiders, ants and bees.

Blessed is blood.  Blessed is the heart.
Blessed are eyes, mouth, ears, hair,

nose, breasts, bellies, legs and feet.
Blessed are all things and all people.

Blessed are sun, moon, stars and rain.
Blessed am I, who lives in blessing.

Blessed are you, child of sun and rain,
embraced by and embracing this world.

# ABOUT THE AUTHOR

Patricia Monaghan passed away on November 11, 2012. She was a Pushcart Prize awarded poet, scholar, spiritual leader, and activist. Patricia had over twenty books published including a geographic and spiritual memoir of Ireland, the Red Haired Girl from the Bog. She published many books of poetry and non-fiction on woman figures connected with the divine. Poetry includes *The Goddess Path, The Goddess Companion,* and *Seasons of the Witch.* Non-fiction includes *Goddesses and Heroines* and editing *Goddesses and World Culture,* a three volume set from authors the world over.

Other works of poetry include *Homefront* a searing collection drawn from personal experience about the effects of war on the veteran's families and *Sanctuary* drawn from times in the West of Ireland and again experience about the Driftless Area of Wisconsin where Patricia lived along with her husband Michael in their land Brigit Rest and where they gardened and tended a vineyard and orchard and processed and preserved the wonders of the land. Non-fiction includes *The Encyclopedia of Irish Mythology, Meditation-The Complete Guide* and *Wineries of Wisconsin and Minnesota* and edited *Brigit, Sun of Womanhood* and *Irish Spirit.*

Patricia finished *Mary, a Novel in Verse* shortly before she died. It represented work done over years and those recently composed to finish the story. This work reflects Patricia's continued immersion of figures from her Irish Catholic upbringing interpreted in a less traditional framework. *Brigit, Sun of Womanhood,* also reflects this immersion and deeper approach, here as saint and earlier, goddess and at present a figure of interest and devotion in many cultures around the world.

Patricia was a professor of inter-disciplinary studies at DePaul University. She was concerned about the lack of spirituality in our society and addressed that in co-founding the Black Earth Institute composed of artists and scholars to direct art in the causes of spirituality, the environment and social justice (www.blackearthinstitute.org). Again to address this issue, this time in relation to academia, she co-founded the Association for the Study of Woman and Mythology to recognize and promote well researched work in the field and to mentor young scholars.

Patricia painted a picture of a different and often better world in her art and not content with that, she created organizations and networks to bring about that picture. She will be missed but her work and love live on. A full list of publications and more information about her may be found at www.patricia.monaghan.com. Michael McDermott, her husband is her literary executor and continues her work.

## Books by Dos Madres Press

Mary Margaret Alvarado - *Hey Folly* (2013)

John Anson - *Jose-Maria de Heredia's Les Trophées* (2013)

Jennifer Arin - *Ways We Hold* (2012)

Michael Autrey - *From The Genre Of Silence* (2008)

Paul Bray - *Things Past and Things to Come* (2006), *Terrible Woods* (2008)

Jon Curley - *New Shadows* (2009), *Angles of Incidents* (2012)

Sara Dailey - *Earlier Lives* (2012)

Dennis Daly - *Nightwalking with Nathaniel-poems of Salem* (2014)

Richard Darabaner - *Plaint* (2012)

Deborah Diemont - *Wanderer* (2009), *Diverting Angels* (2012)

Joseph Donahue - *The Copper Scroll* (2007)

Annie Finch - *Home Birth* (2004)

Norman Finkelstein - *An Assembly* (2004), *Scribe* (2009)

Gerry Grubbs - *Still Life* (2005), *Girls in Bright Dresses Dancing* (2010),
    *The Hive-a book we read for its honey* (2013)

Ruth D. Handel - *Tugboat Warrior* (2013)

Richard Hague - *Burst, Poems Quickly* (2004),
    *During The Recent Extinctions* (2012)

Pauletta Hansel - *First Person* (2007), *What I Did There* (2011)

Michael Heller - *A Look at the Door with the Hinges Off* (2006),
    *Earth and Cave* (2006)

Michael Henson - *The Tao of Longing & The Body Geographic* (2010)

R. Nemo Hill - *When Men Bow Down* (2012)

W. Nick Hill - *And We'd Understand Crows Laughing* (2012)

Eric Hoffman - *Life At Braintree* (2008), *The American Eye* (2011),
    *By The Hours* (2013)

James Hogan - *Rue St. Jacques* (2005)

Keith Holyoak - *My Minotaur* (2010), *Foreigner* (2012)

Nancy Kassell - *Text(isles)* (2013)

David M. Katz - *Claims of Home* (2011)

Sherry Kearns - *Deep Kiss* (2013)

Burt Kimmelman - *There Are Words* (2007), *The Way We Live* (2011)

Ralph La Charity - *Farewellia a la Aralee* (2014)

Pamela L. Laskin - *Plagiarist* (2012)

Owen Lewis - *Sometimes Full of Daylight* (2013)

Richard Luftig - *Off The Map* (2006)

Austin MacRae - *The Organ Builder* (2012)

Mario Markus - *Chemical Poems-One For Each Element* (2013)

J. Morris - *The Musician, Approaching Sleep* (2006)

Rick Mullin - *Soutine* (2012), *Coelacanth* (2013)

Robert Murphy - *Not For You Alone* (2004), *Life in the Ordovician* (2007),
    *From Behind The Blind* (2013)

Pam O'Brien - *The Answer To Each Is The Same* (2012)

Peter O'Leary - *A Mystical Theology of the Limbic Fissure* (2005)

Bea Opengart - *In The Land* (2011)

David A. Petreman - *Candlelight in Quintero - bilingual edition* (2011)

Paul Pines - *Reflections in a Smoking Mirror* (2011), *New Orleans Variations*
    *& Paris Ouroboros* (2013)

David Schloss - *Behind the Eyes* (2005)

William Schickel - *What A Woman* (2007)

Lianne Spidel & Anne Loveland - *Pairings* (2012)

Murray Shugars - *Songs My Mother Never Taught Me* (2011),
    *Snakebit Kudzu* (2013)

Jason Shulman - *What does reward bring you but to bind you to Heaven*
    *like a slave? (2013)*

Olivia Stiffler - *Otherwise, we are safe* (2013)

Carole Stone - *Hurt, the Shadow- the Josephine Hopper poems* (2013)

Nathan Swartzendruber - *Opaque Projectionist* (2009)

Jean Syed - *Sonnets* (2009)

Madeline Tiger - *The Atheist's Prayer* (2010), *From the Viewing Stand* (2011)

James Tolan - *Red Walls* (2011)

Brian Volck - *Flesh Becomes Word* (2013)

Henry Weinfield - *The Tears of the Muses* (2005),
    *Without Mythologies* (2008), *A Wandering Aramaean* (2012)

Donald Wellman - *A North Atlantic Wall* (2010),
    *The Cranberry Island Series* (2012)

Anne Whitehouse - *The Refrain* (2012)

Martin Willetts Jr. - *Secrets No One Must Talk About* (2011)

Tyrone Williams - *Futures, Elections* (2004), *Adventures of Pi* (2011)

Kip Zegers - *The Poet of Schools* (2013)

www.dosmadres.com